AF198885

COFFEE SHOP DIARIES

II

j. t. baka

At Tully's

no. 4

I

I

can't say

I

tried something

new

even

when I was

still human

I

wasn't what

was requiered

I

was just me

which wasn't that

bad

don't get me wrong

it was enough

to spark some interest

at least

at least here

in this very city

on a rainy day

just look

ame

II

didn't follow

the pied piper to that one

funny how things

turn out sometimes

looking for her movies

or some merchandise

and then

meeting her in the subway

twice in one day

but

I am here for the third time

written on the third day

of my stay

exactly

two months after

my father's death

in the year of my 30th JT anniversary

I didn't want to go

away

no way

I want to

stay

III

clouds on the rainy side

of the river

a few drops

of blood

splattered on the wood

of the bridge

over the river

after a sword

cut through the light blue

of the sky

on the sunny side

of the river

while I was sitting

at tully's

trying to be

human

by eating

a slice of heaven

IV

a big wave

is crushing into the red mountain

awakening

a celestial dragon

from its deep slumber

of a thousand years

climbing in its chariot

of thunder

the dragon is riding the skies

raiding the castles of air

for their maidens

I saw it in a painting

in the palace

of the cloud's emperor

V

the woodblock printing

came alive

the dancers

the wagons

the people crowding the streets

I even heard the music playing

in my mind

just before the rain washed away

all ink and turned the paper

into mush

VI

places

you have to go

temple

school

bridge

aqueduct

arashiyama area

gion

kyoto tower

and *kyoto station*

or in one simple word

MAIKO

no. 5

VII

I

came that late

I

was the only one

a car

just for myself

into the night

the streets just

like that

just for me

empty

empty like

myself

after finishing

business

after finished

business

after

me

VIII

when I

came back from

where I

am now

it felt

right

it was the right

thing to do

looking at it

from

where I am now

I am

not so sure anymore

I know

why I am here

but I

don't feel like it

maybe I am

not me anymore

maybe

I moved on

shit happens

you know

IX

the world

is upside

down

but you don't

care

not because you

are a hare

and wouldn't even

try to dare

the nightmare

or imagine

black ships arriving

at the shore

to score

no

in your case

maybe a peach might come

flying

crying

at the uttermost

but

on second thoughts

that's not

that kind of show

so that's not the reason for any treason

it's just

look at you

906

for you

the world is never

going to be

upside down

906

for you

everything is always true

for you

the world is always free jazz

that's my guess

X

didn't know

what to do

on a rainy day

but what can you do

on a rainy day in Kyoto

you can try

to re-enact a snowy day

and end up

buying art supplies for painting

which is prohibited there anyway

but no

you end up

buying a print of black ships

at the store

in which he did buy the art supplies

for her

but you

you are buying it just for you

because this is not a movie

obviously

it's just for a poem on a rainy day

which is also a 13th

which is also a friday

and on which

mother sent her greetings too

welcome the arrival of the black ships

on this rainy day

with one *gitanes*

my son

XI

on top of the mountain

a plateau overlooking the city

one chimera of a tree

and me sitting in its shadow

while all around

ghosts are dancing

past lives

loves lost

I still feel

the phantom kisses

on my lips

a shower of falling stars

covering the nightsky

shattered hopes

it was a new day yesterday

oh josefine

I can still hear you

calling

let's dance

I can still see you

coming down

on me

still

taking my hand

we start to twirl

higher and higher

still

until

we disolve

into the night

together

still

XII

under a full moon

an army of bloodthirsty kamis

is marching through

the togokumen

all around them

golden stardust

is glittering through the night

ready to battle

ready to kill

ready to drink the blood of their enemies

they are

while high up in the clouds

behind the walls of air

a thousand lizards

are dreaming

dreaming they are

of a hightowering wave of black unicorns

hate dripping off their deadly horns

coming in full force

ready to strike

ready to kill

surrounding

the frightened dragon of kei

they are waiting for the right moment

ready to let go

ready to kill

they are waiting

for the lizards to awaken

as one

as the frightening dragon of ai

the greatest of all wizards

talll and small

they are waiting

impatiently

for him to free them

from this dream

and lead them on

lead them on

to fight the army of kamis

to drench the nightsky in their blood

to quench their own thirst

for blood

no. 6

XIII

josefine

was a mouse

one day

she was running for her life

she was

chased by a cat

josefine

was fast

but

the cat was fast as well

josefine

was running there

josefine

was running here

josefine

was running all over the place

josefine

was good at that

but

the cat was good in her job as well

in the end

josefine was running up a couple of steps

and there

was a gate

the gate

was shut

josefine stopped

and threw glances left and right

there and everywhere

were mountains of bricks

josefine

was cornered

panic-stricken

she turned around and round and round

she

turned around

finally facing

the cat

the cat

was smiling

josefine

was staring into rows of rows of very sharp
teeth

josefine

started to cry

josefine

started to sing

josefine

sang about her predicament

josefine

sang about her misery which was no
mystery

josefine

was quite good at that

the cat

instead of eating her at once listened

but in the end

the cat cut josefine off

but instead of making it quick

the cat gave josefine advice first

on the steps

there was a man

maybe his name was Aqualung

I'm not sure

he was living there

on the steps

he was living there

right next to the gate

and like the cat he

had also listened to josefine singing

when

he heard the cat's advice

when

he heard what the cat had to say

he couldn't keep quiet

any longer

for he

felt the same as josefine

so he said to josefine

they were in the same boat

like she was

he was trapped

trapped by

the keeper of the gate

to make his point he was pointing

to the big man standing next to the other
side of the gate

josefine

was looking from the poor man to the giant
gate keeper

josefine

didn't know what to say and said therefore
nothing

the keeper of the gate

had listened to josefine singing and the man
lamenting

the keeper of the gate

had said nothing

but now

the keeper of the gate was snorting

he looked straight

at the man and at josefine

you are both wrong

he said

wrong you are both

he said

both of you just fell for the wrong lies

he said

because it was convenient for you

he said

and the cat listening to him

was nodding her consent

while

josefine and the man looked at each other

confused and shocked

and maybe even betrayed

realizing the truth

of the keeper's words

they died

a good death

XIV

the blow

wasn't for show

for sure

it wasn't the cure

but sometimes dope

is the best hope

and it's quite clear

don't search for a tear

in a glass full of bear

tearing up

clearing up

who knows

who shows

true colours

is there a rhyme

maybe dollars

quickly before I turn

sickly

prong

please sing a song

to make not just me better

in this matter

we don't need a reason

for treason

just have fun

and it is perfectly done

so many seals

on summerday sands

so many squeals

let's dance

looking for direction

there is too much distraction

make it bright

so we will be alright

forever

or

never

XV

in the morning

the streets almost empty

in the morning

the sun came and went

in the morning

dark clouds in one direction

and in another a blue sky

later that day

so many faces

later that day

so often it was

I could understand

what people were saying

I felt out of place

later that day

the coffee shop was overcrowded

I went shopping instead of writing

and there she was

and not

in the subway this time

I took the chance

XVI

in the heart of winter

near the fireside

a guitar is sleeping

curious

the fire is watching the guitar

touching

so lightly

her strings with its light

the guitar sighs

velvet notes

are filling the big hall

smothing the cold

something inside the fire

stirs

the fire's light growing brighter

caressing the guitar

the guitar moanes

stirs without waking up

through a window

the wind is watching

the wind itself is curious

watching the fire playing

the wind grows restless

restless like the fire

until it can't restrain itself

no longer and pushes open

the window into the hall

the wind pushes the fire to the side

to play the guitar for itself

but all the wind does

is fueling the fire's desire

fueling its rage

the fire is snatching

the guitar by her neck

seizing her

turning up the heat

which fuels the wind's envy and jealousy

the guitar screams in her dreams

the wind trys

to take hold of the guitar

while the fire plays ever so wildly

until the wind turns into a storm

stomping out the fire

stomping out the light

filling the winter's heart with darkness

forever

silencing the guitar

for good

no. 7

XVII

while I was

ready for boarding

the gate was not

waiting for the gate

to get ready

I was watching people

there was a woman

she was sitting

down sipping

a cup of coffee

at one time

she got up leaving

her cup behind

there it was

in plain view

for everyone to see

alone

for me

it was a mystery

solved

I always wondered

how those abandoned cups

ended up the way they did

now

I know

but that

was not

the end of it

the woman came back

after a while

sitting down

she grabed the cup of coffee

and started to sip at it again

as it was nothing special

the normal thing to do

you know

as if

she never went away

in front of the gate

was a coffee shop

when I arrived at the gate

I went there and ordered

a caramel macchiato iced

I had the feeling

the barista and I

were flirting

the sleeve around my cup

definitely cried

LOVE

I am wondering

what will happen

if I go to the coffee shop again

before my next trip

what will happen

when I go back

to her

will it be the same

as the woman coming back

to her cup of coffee

XVIII

the bride of the night

felt alright

and turned on the light

but the light

was too bright

and her groom

looked like a buffon

so all he could do

was to turn into

a groom of doom

and then he got cocky

and her love went wild and rocky

but they didn't desist

because they couldn't resist

their love was big

you know

not just for show

it wasn't an act

indeed it was a fact

and because

they felt desired

they were inspired

doom night

night doom

beautiful children of bride and groom

XIX

after coming back to korea

I met a friend for lunch

after lunch

we went

for a cup of coffee at starbucks

before I could order

the barista there greeted me

with a *long time no see*

she was wearing a face mask

as we were living in the time

of covid-19

she was also wearing

a starbucks hat as well

I didn't recongnize her

at all

maybe because

maybe because

I was confused

I didn't know

anybody at starbucks

at starbucks in seoul

at least

I didn't do my thing

with women working

at starbucks

in seoul

did it matter

did it matter

that it was a starbucks

near my former workplace

that area

that place

was a twosome place

once

her name tag said
apple

the temptation
I resistet

I didn't
bite

XX

on a rainy day

pilgramage to the turtle's well

place of their first meeting

on a rainy day

pilgramage to the bamboo grove

place of their second promise

on a rainy day

pilgramage to the pottery store

place of their first promise

an owl in snow

was waiting

on a rainy day

passing of the sports supplies dealer

where they said yesterday

they didn't know

when the new jersey of *Kyoto Sanga*

will be on sale

today

it was

on sale and mine

while hiding from the rain

strolling through teramachi

while passing shops with ukiyo-e

the pa played a soundtrack I knew

the umbrellas of cherbourgh

on a rainy day

in the city of *virgin snow*

after *days of being wild*

I expected *doctor zhivago*

at least

in the mood for love

I was in

on a rainy day

XXI

under cover

of rain

behind

a mask

I see

people floating by

on their pressure

on their stress

on their dreams

I hear

only the silent

scream

who are

hiding in the shadows

of their successes

who are

advertising

their failures

who is

stopping the knife

of loving you

when the window of opportunity

is smashed in

and everything inside

your soul

defiled

XXII

not

nana

not

nanae

deers instead

and

so many

of them

guarding a gigantic bronze buddha

in an even more gigantic wooden hall

but beauty

awaits

in a museum so modern

with guerilla tunnels

instead of exhibition halls

not the art of war

but the war for art

still

the beauty is

there

unlike other places

post^n

the world one

after rei ayanami's

where you can't fuck up

an order

for a cup of coffee

at tully's in arashiyama

bakaru

XXIII

cloudy

in the morning

but with

a ray of light

italien greetings

the clock

is ticking

tomorrow tomorrow

see the sorrow

the infection rate

rising

sometimes

it's good

to be a guy

in between

a guy

alone and lost

nothing

will find me in the void

of a deserted heart

inside the closet

I am safe

as death

XXIV

it wasn't the rain

we were waiting for

it wasn't the snow

long extinct

we were waiting for

it wasn't even the virus

we were waiting for

it was already here

it was the fallout of the pain

we anticipated

with dread

only the dead will rise

so they say

but we

we never lived

XXV

the cloud

was shy

it took

the cloud

a long

time to

come out

of hiding

behind a

huge rock

but luckily

the sun

was still

waiting for

the cloud

so finally

they met

and happily

the cloud

was crying

the cloud

cried for

a long

long time

but when

the fox

and the

deer encountered

each other

and fell

for each

other deeply

the rain

finally stopped

that's how

amayame

was born

epilogue.think coffee 2

vienna

via dusseldorf

to incheon

incheon

via osaka

to **KYOTO**

from babymetal

to MAIKO

that was the plan

KYOTO

via osaka

to incheon

now what

now

think

carefully

that is

what you are here for

again

aren't you

Credits

Writer: j. t. baka.

Written (analogue): from the 3rd of July 2019 to the 26th of February 2020.

Written (digital): from the 7th of February 2020 to the 1st of March 2020.

Pictures: Simon Wagenschütz.

Editorial deadline (lyrics): the 3rd of June 2020.

IN MEMORIAM

Impressum

Redaktionsschluss: 23.07.2020.

©2020 baka, j. t.
Herstellung und Verlag: BoD - Books on Demand,
Norderstedt.

ISBN-13: 9783751951371.